Ancient Egyptian Art

by Grace Hansen

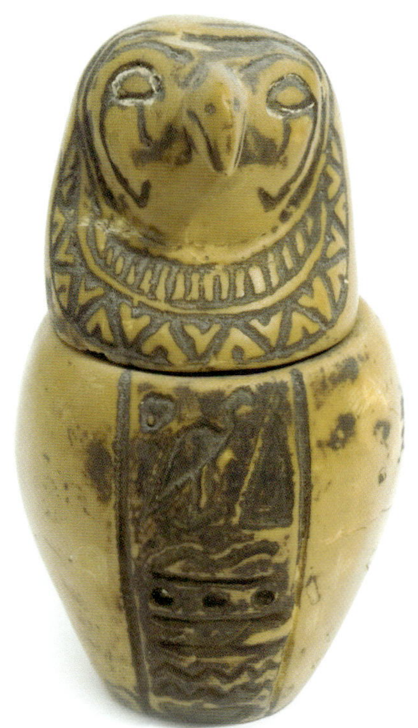

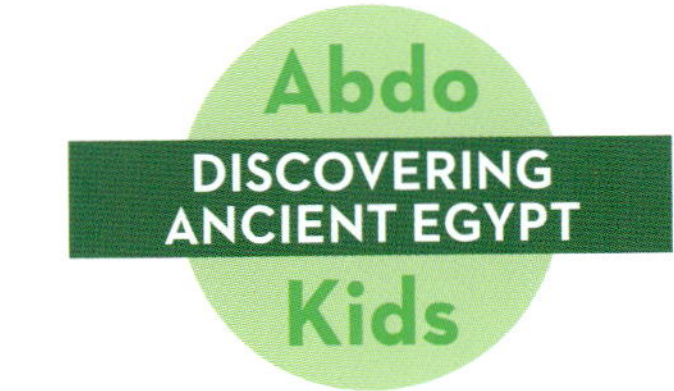

Abdo Kids Jumbo is an Imprint of Abdo Kids
abdobooks.com

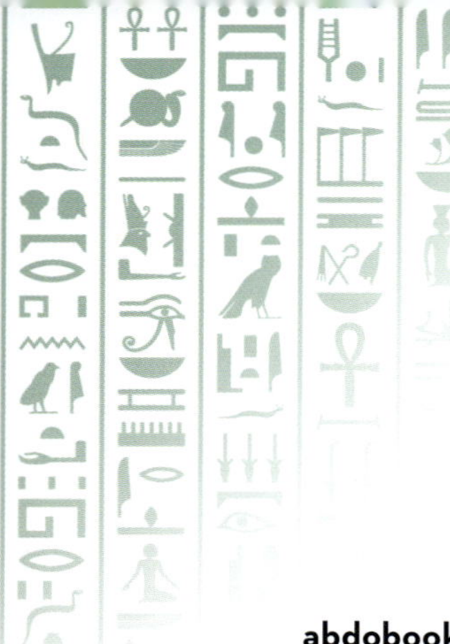

abdobooks.com

Published by Abdo Kids, a division of ABDO, P.O. Box 398166, Minneapolis, Minnesota 55439.

Abdo Kids Jumbo™ is a trademark and logo of Abdo Kids.

Printed in the United States of America, North Mankato, Minnesota.

102023

012024

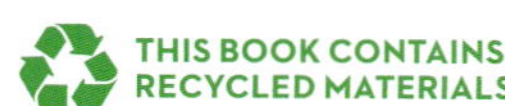

Photo Credits: Alamy, Getty Images, Shutterstock

Production Contributors: Teddy Borth, Jennie Forsberg, Grace Hansen
Design Contributors: Victoria Bates, Candice Keimig

Library of Congress Control Number: 2023937684

Publisher's Cataloging-in-Publication Data

Names: Hansen, Grace, author.

Title: Ancient Egyptian art / by Grace Hansen

Description: Minneapolis, Minnesota : Abdo Kids, 2024 | Series: Discovering ancient Egypt | Includes online resources and index.

Identifiers: ISBN 9781098268428 (lib. bdg.) | ISBN 9781098269128 (ebook) | ISBN 9781098269470 (Read-to-Me ebook)

Subjects: LCSH: Art, Ancient--Egypt--Juvenile literature. | Art and anthropology--Juvenile literature. | Egypt--History--Juvenile literature.

Classification: DDC 932--dc23

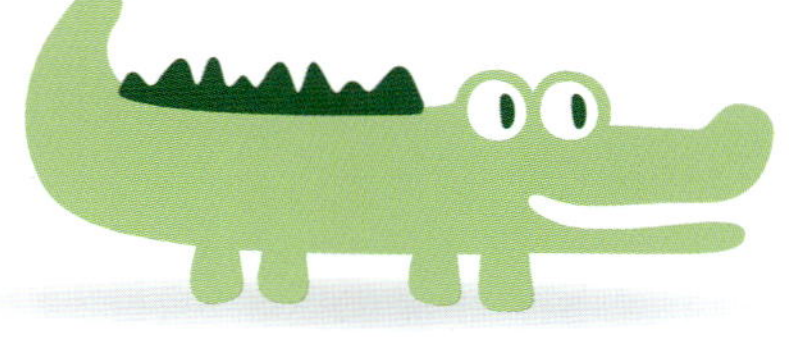

Table of Contents

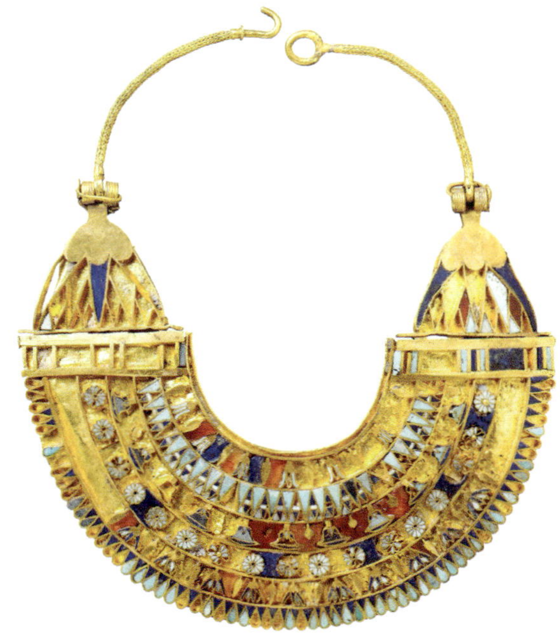

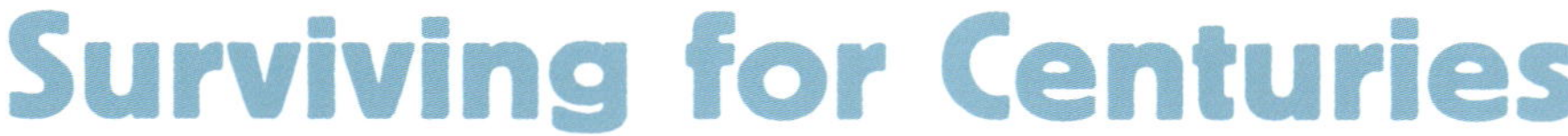

Surviving for Centuries

Surviving ancient Egyptian art gives people a look back in time. It shows us how the ancient Egyptians lived. It also helps us understand their religion and what was important to them.

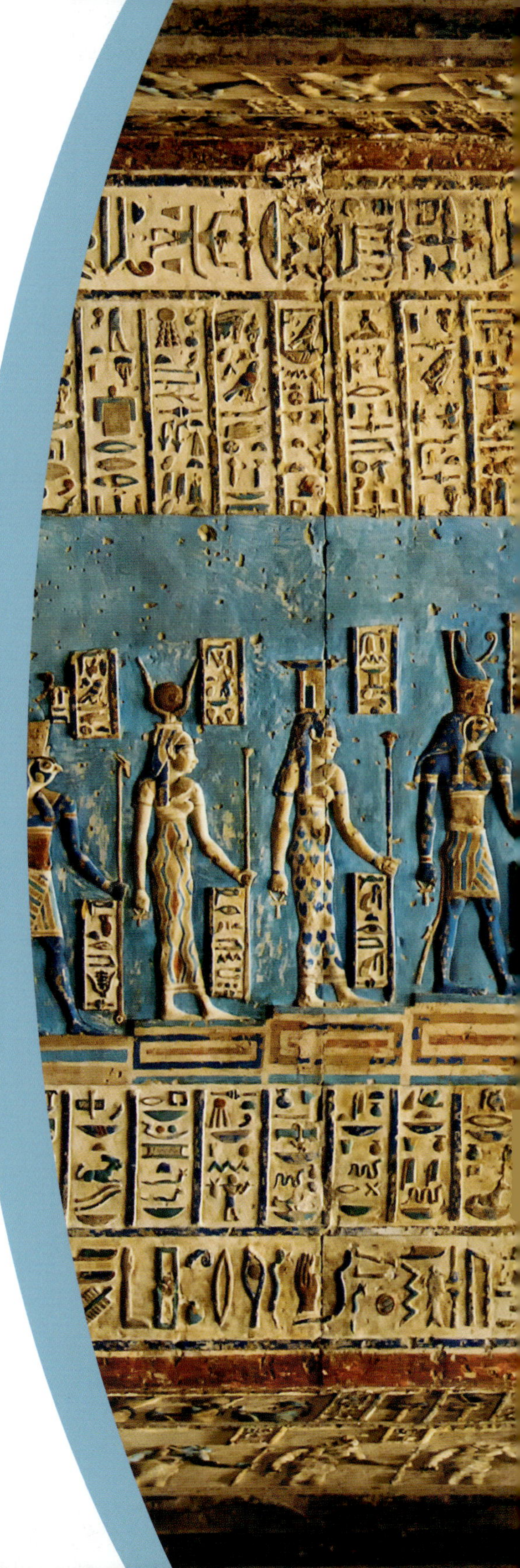

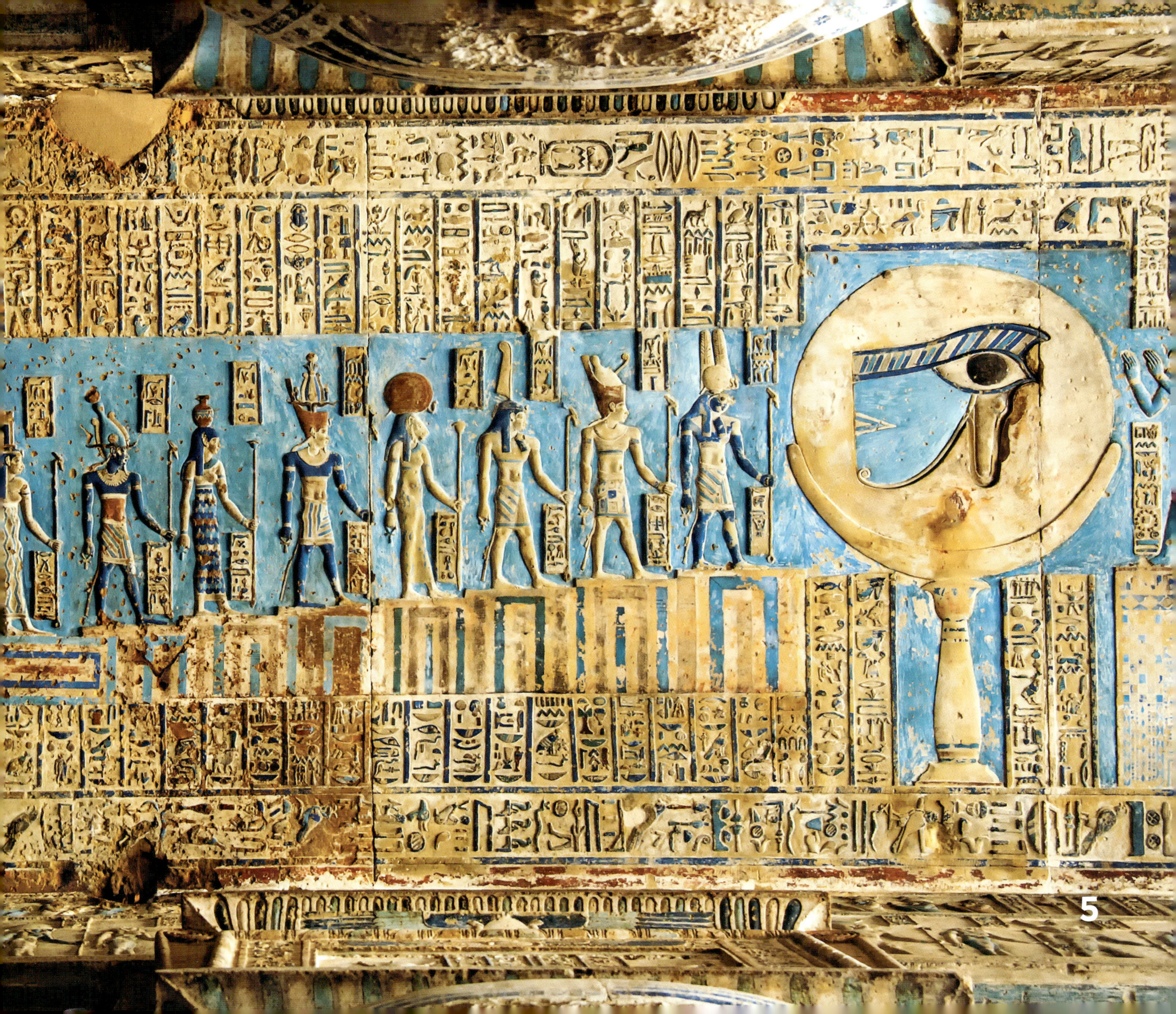

5

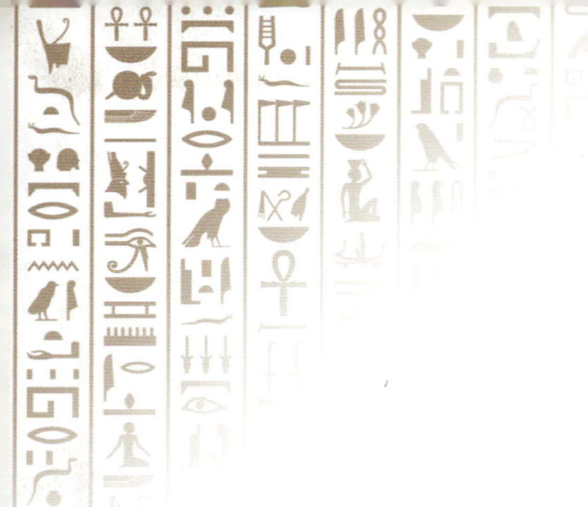

Ancient Egyptian art was created between 3150 BCE and 30 BCE. It has survived for more than 2,000 years! This is mainly due to Egypt's dry **climate**.

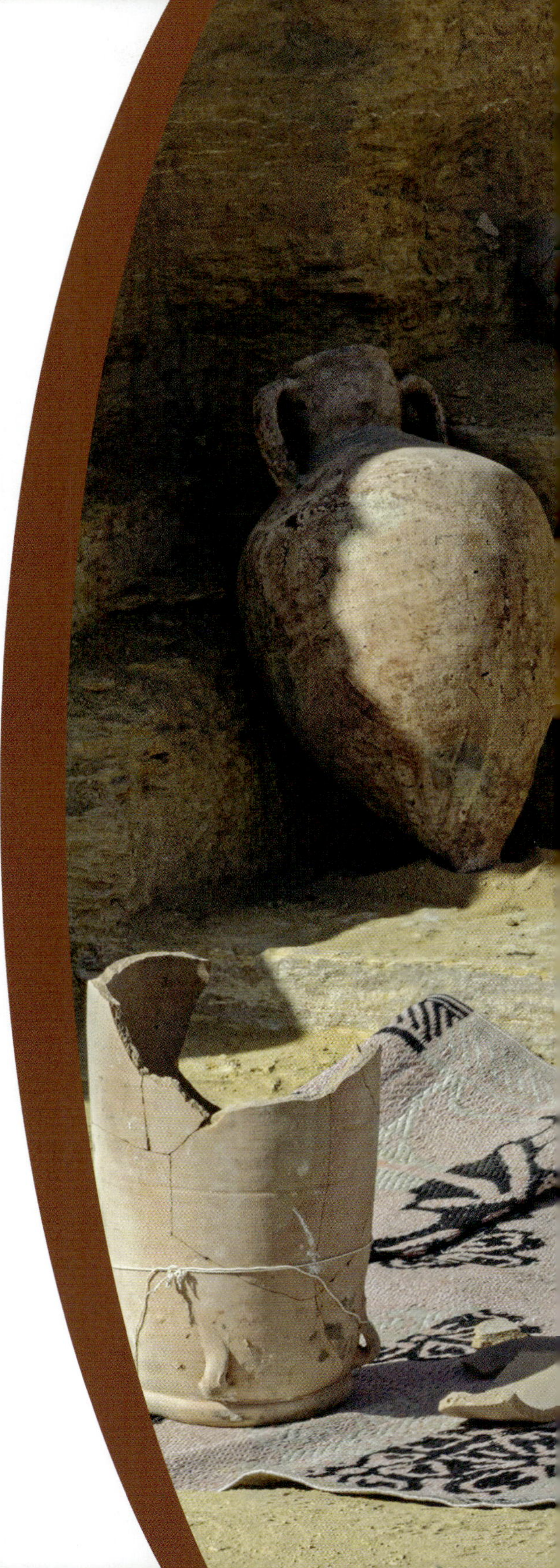

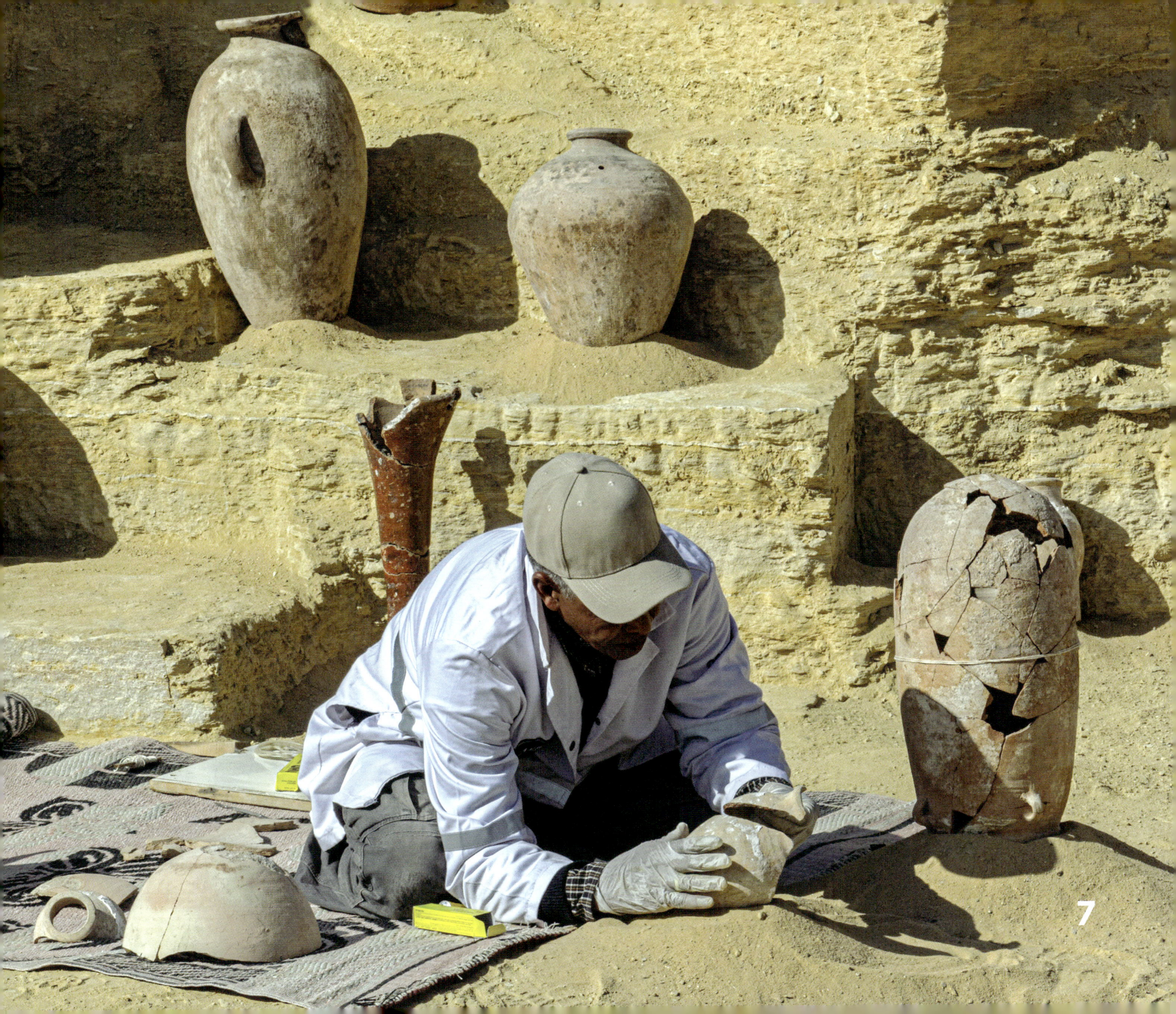
7

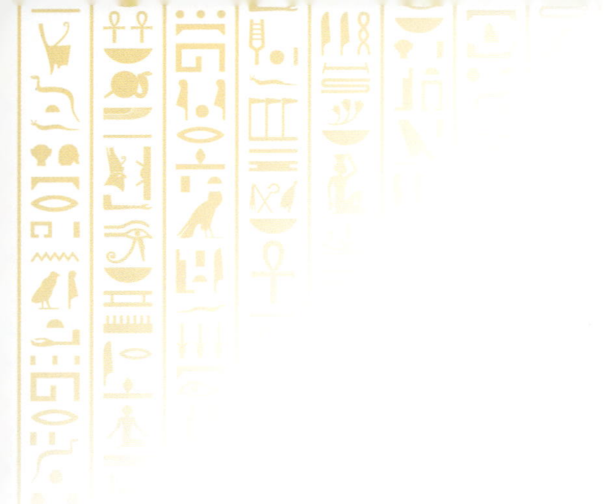

Ancient Egyptian art comes in many forms. These include pottery, glasswork, jewelry, and paintings.

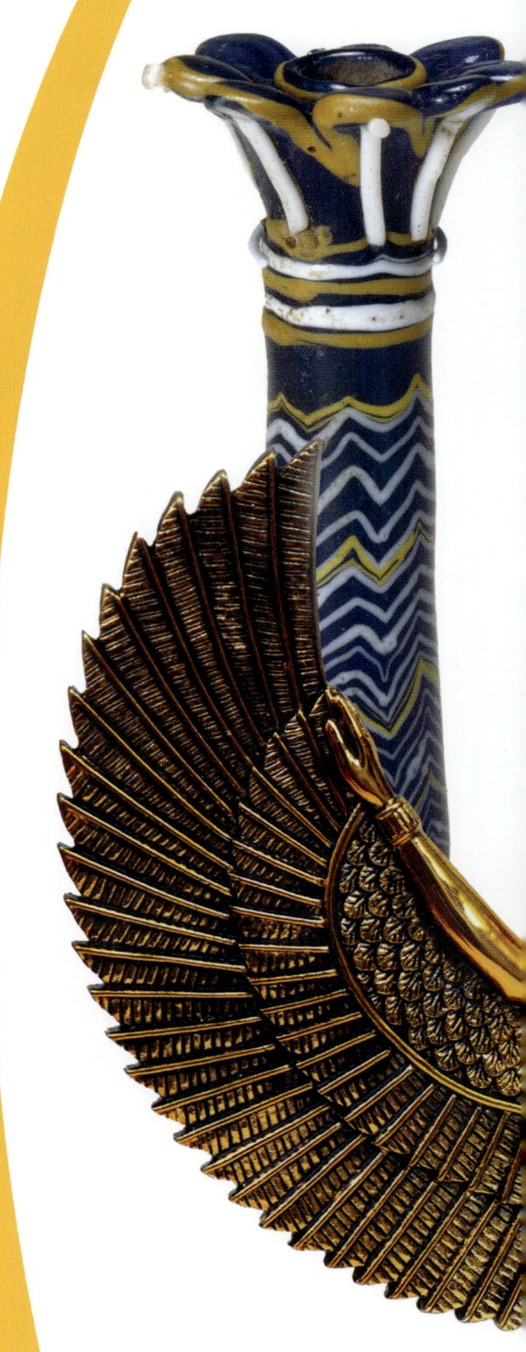

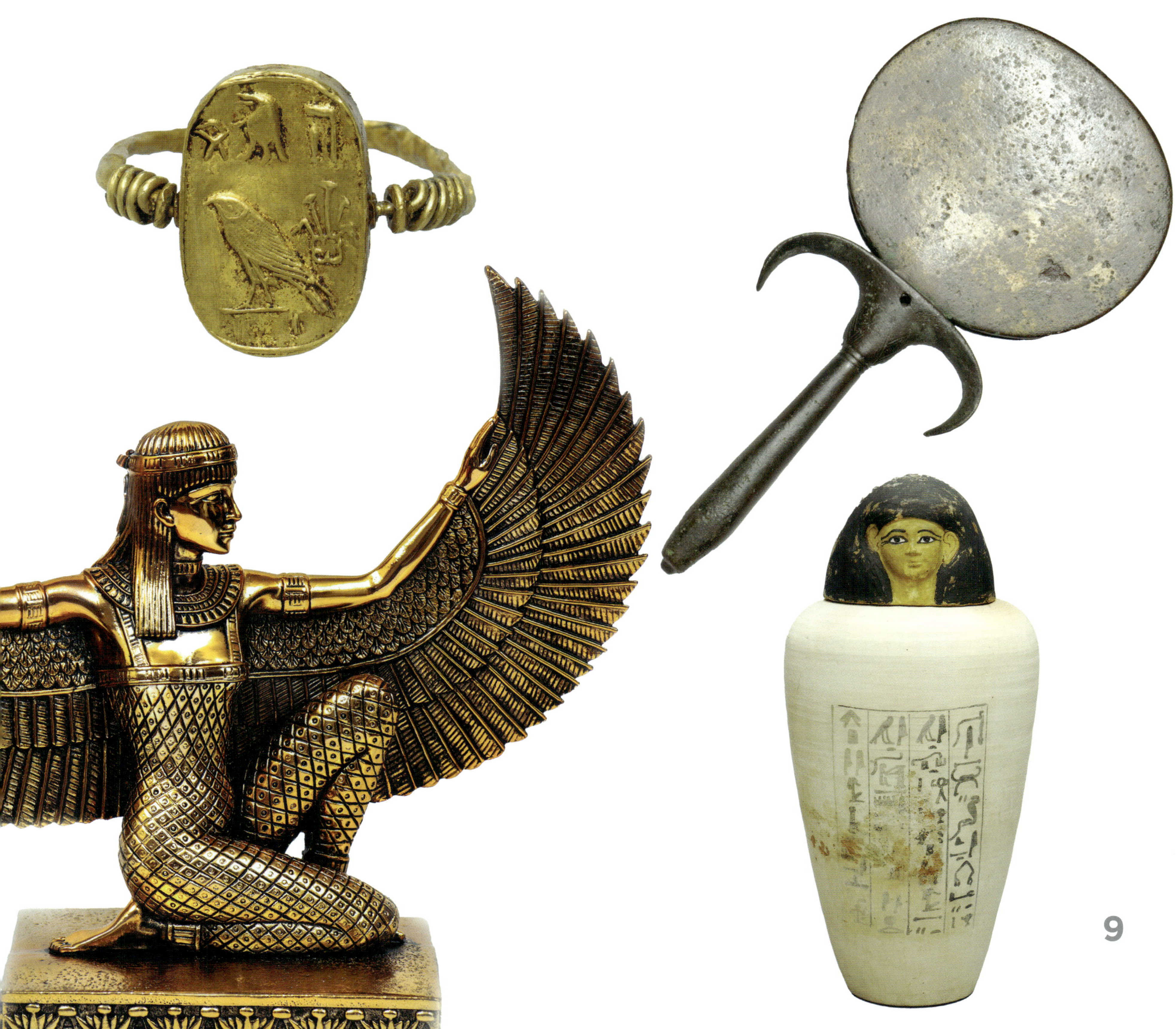

Pottery

The ancient Egyptians used clay to make pottery. Potters shaped pots by hand or on a potter's wheel. The pots were then baked. Beginning in the 500s BCE, the Egyptians learned to **glaze**.

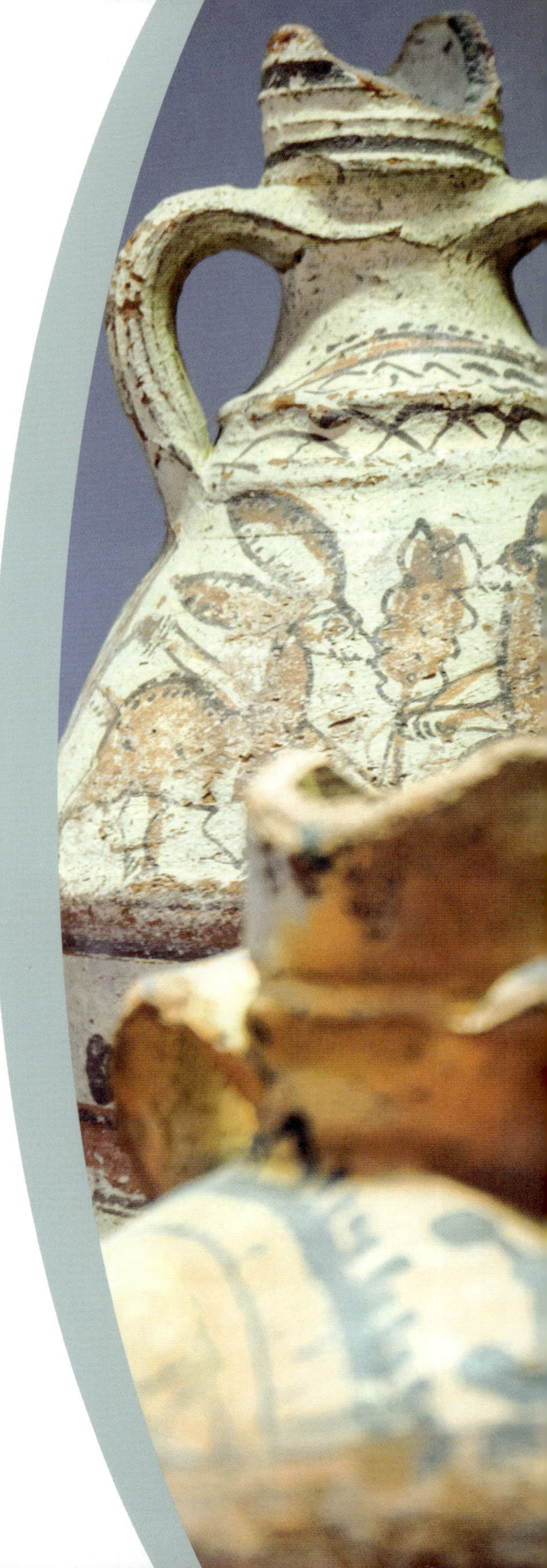

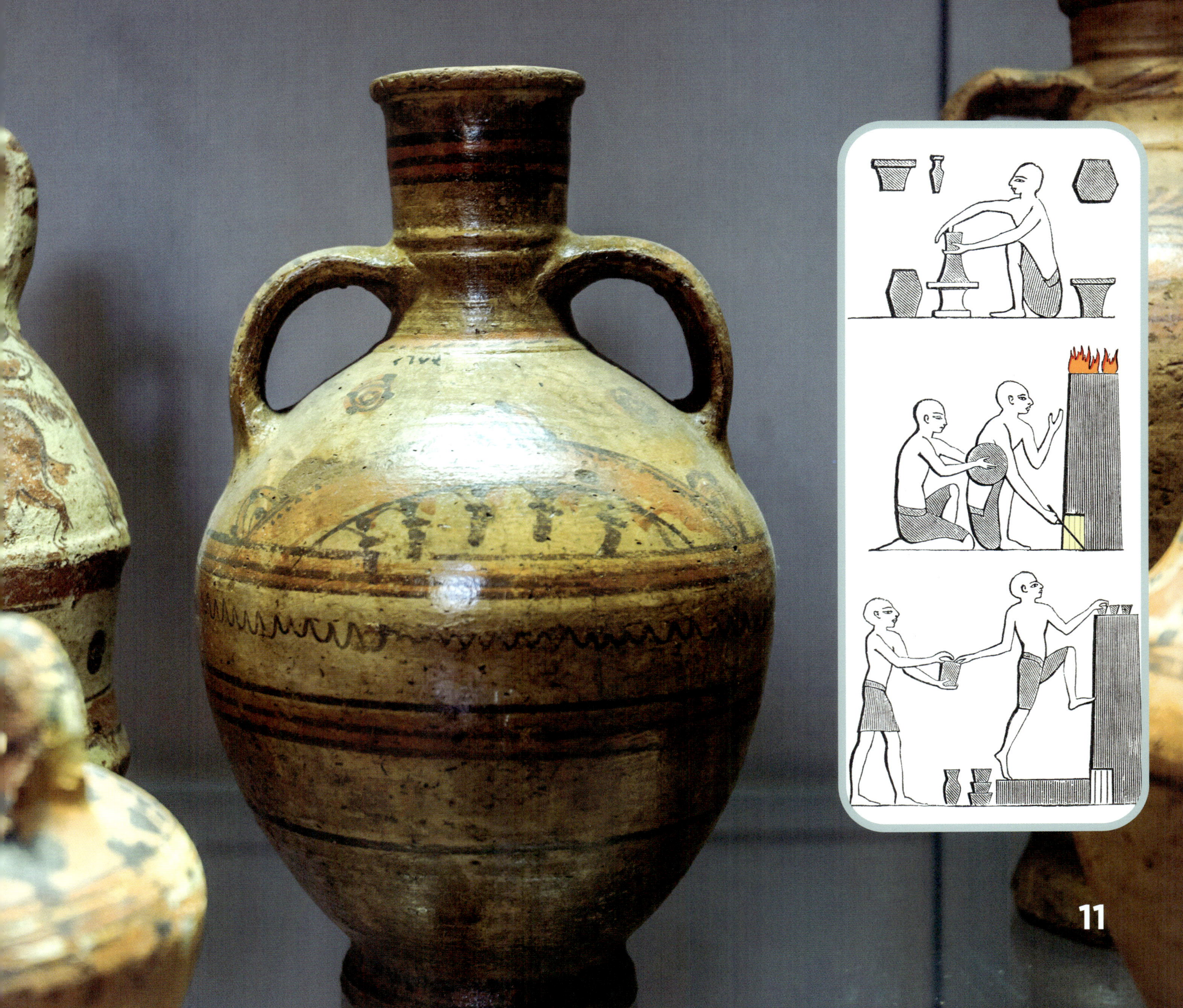

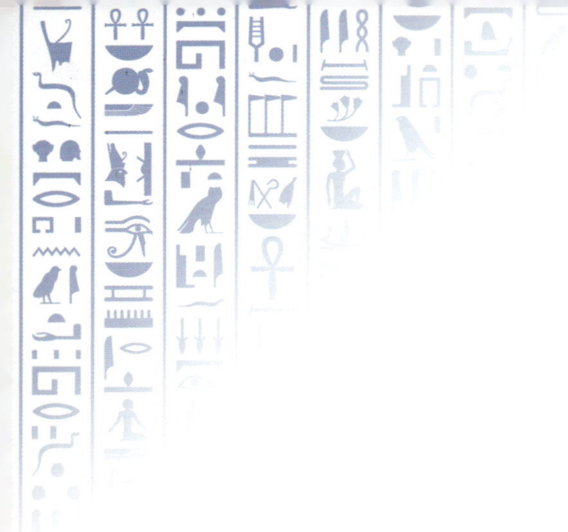

Egyptian **faience** is another type of pottery. Potters made a paste that could be shaped into jewelry and other decorative objects.

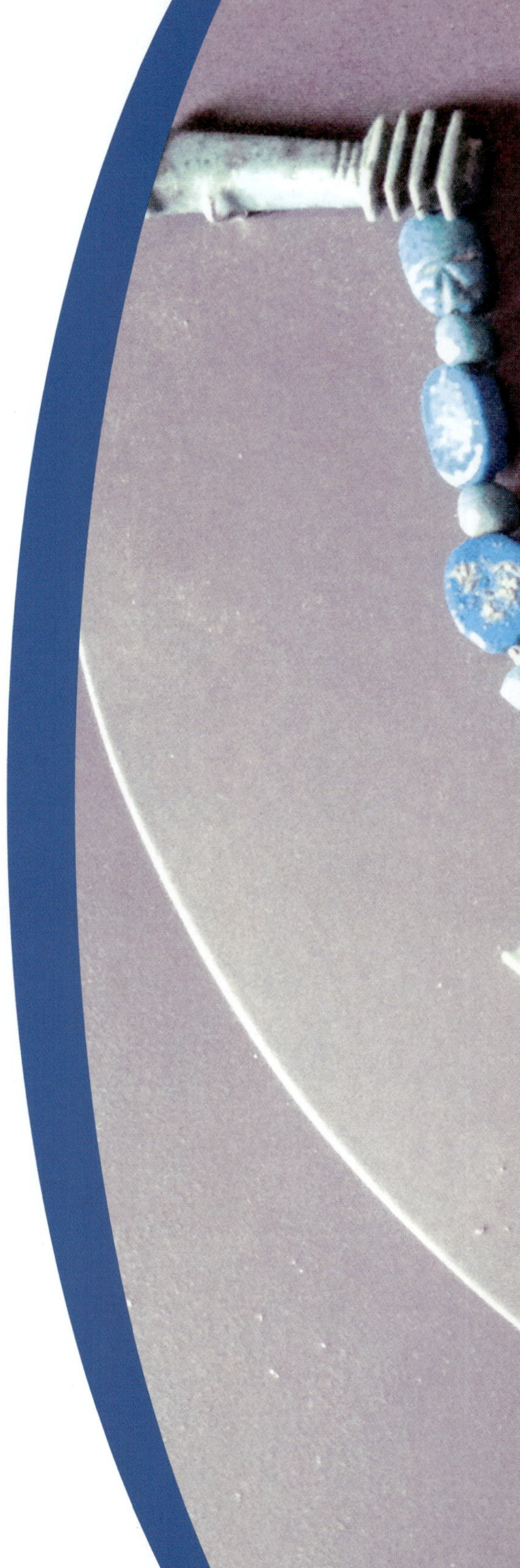

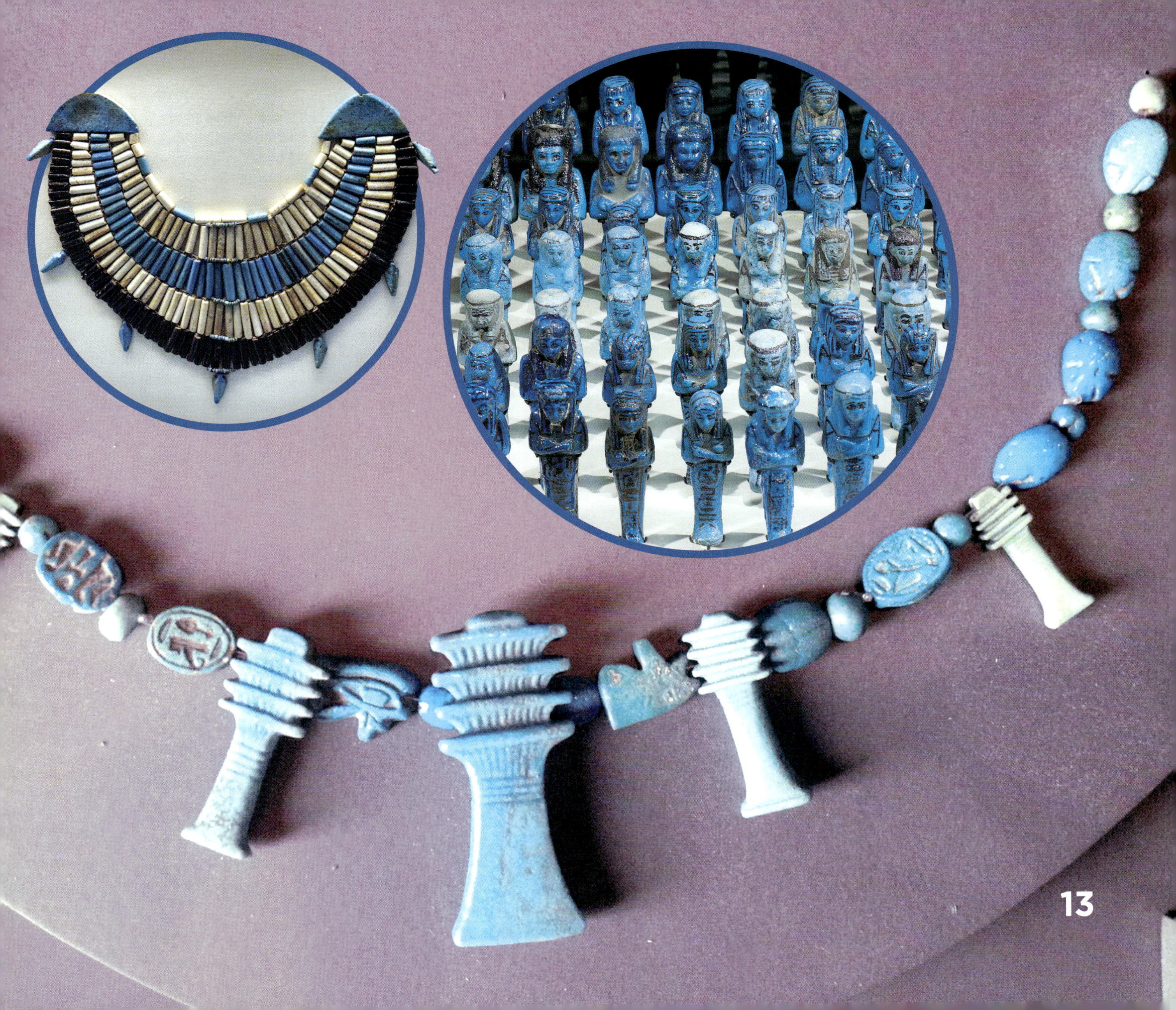

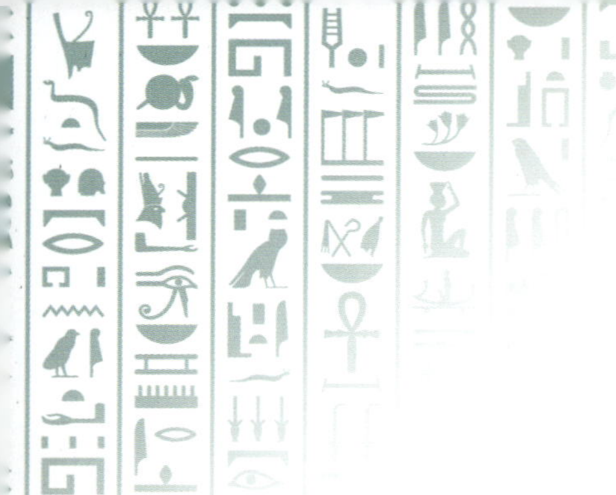

Glass & Jewelry

The ancient Egyptians created beautiful glass objects. They used molds to shape molten, colored glass. Glass was used to make beads, figures, tiles, and other items.

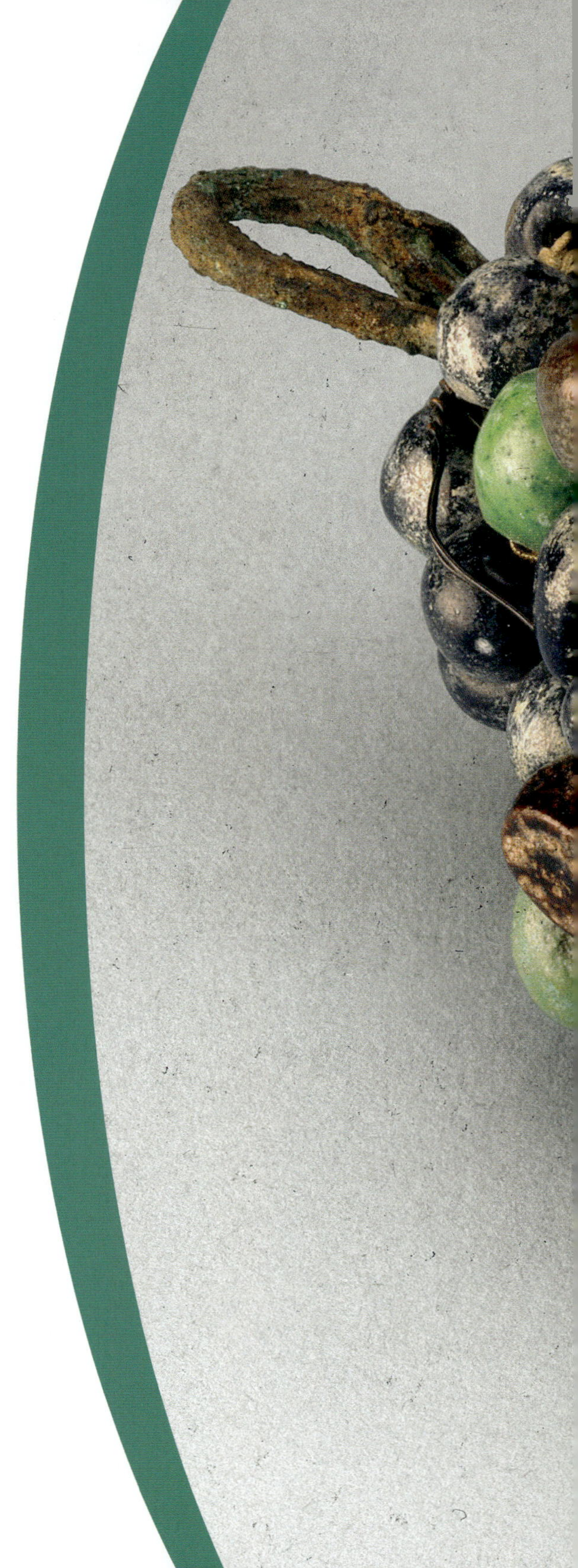

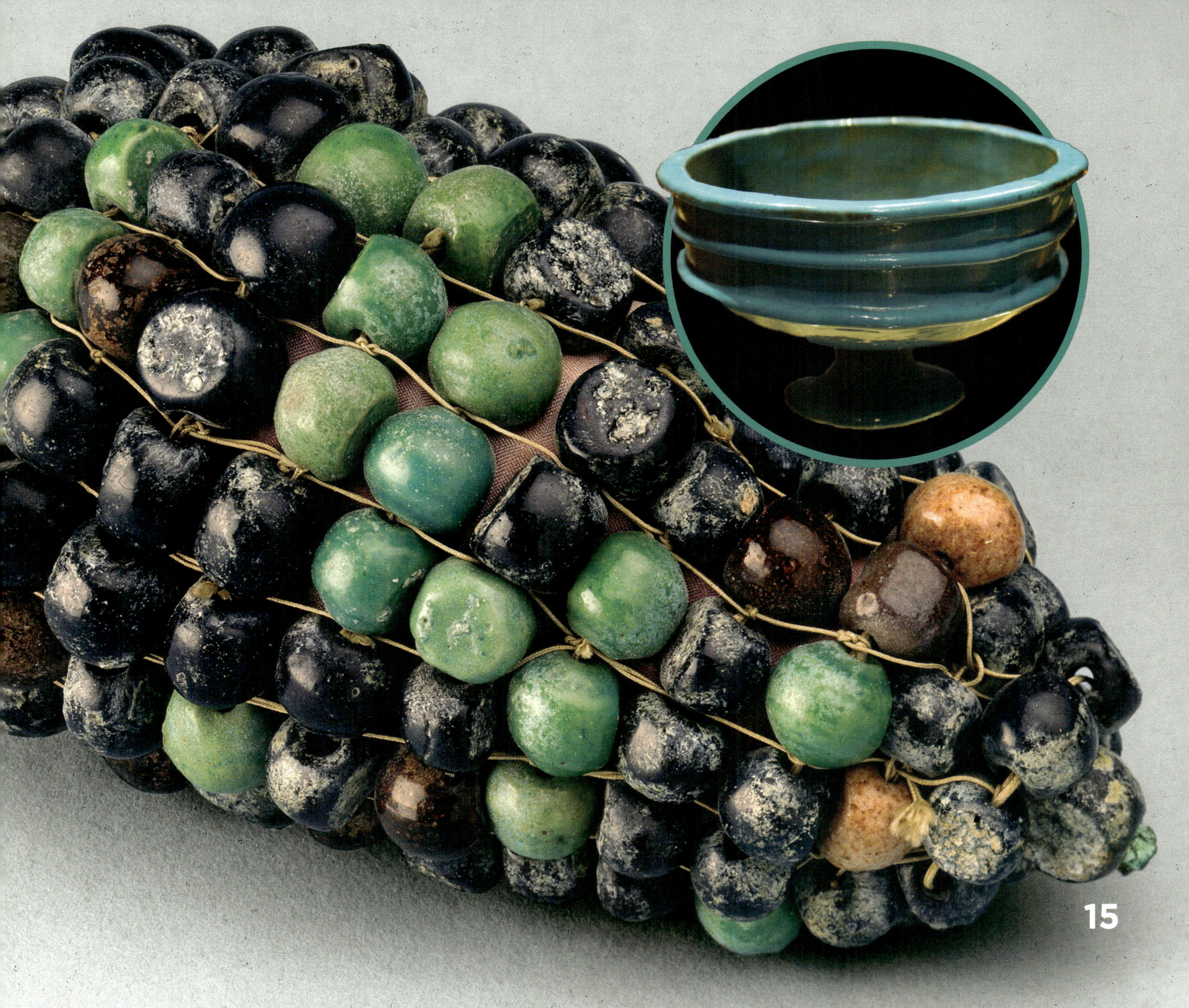

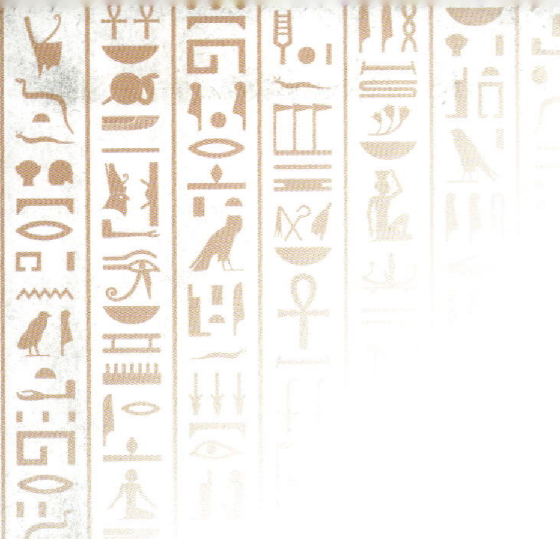

Artisans crafted jewelry such as pendants, collars, and cuffs. Every ancient Egyptian, no matter their place in society, wore jewelry.

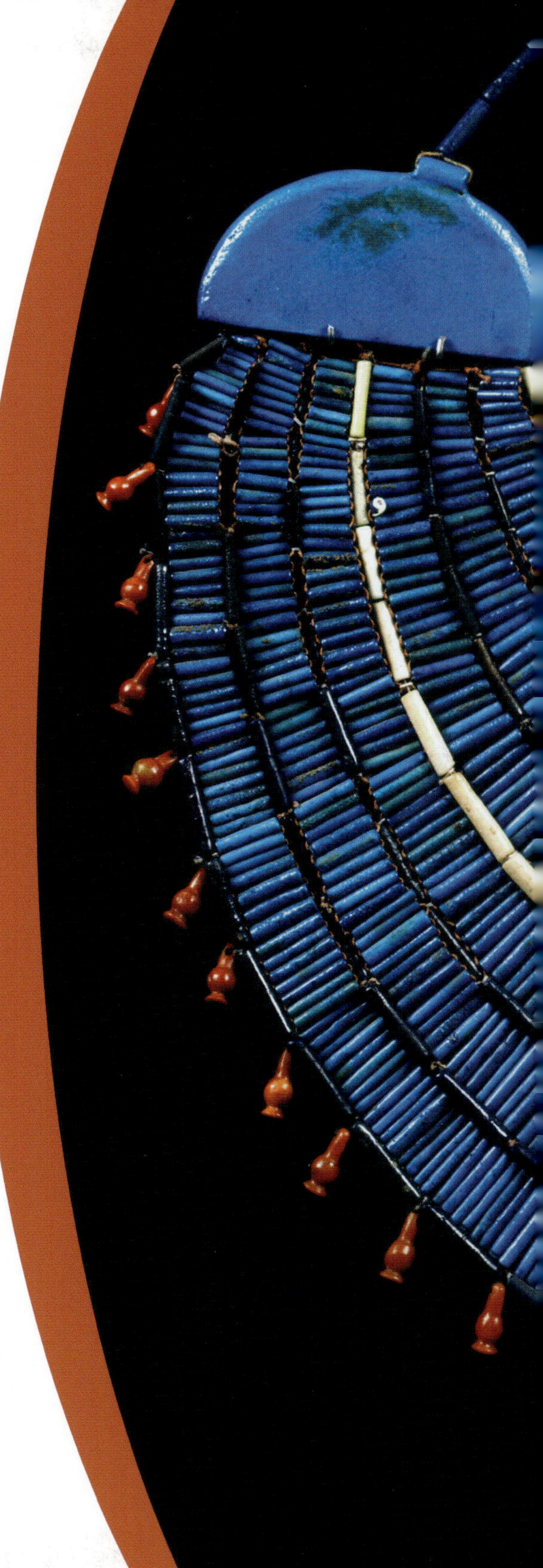

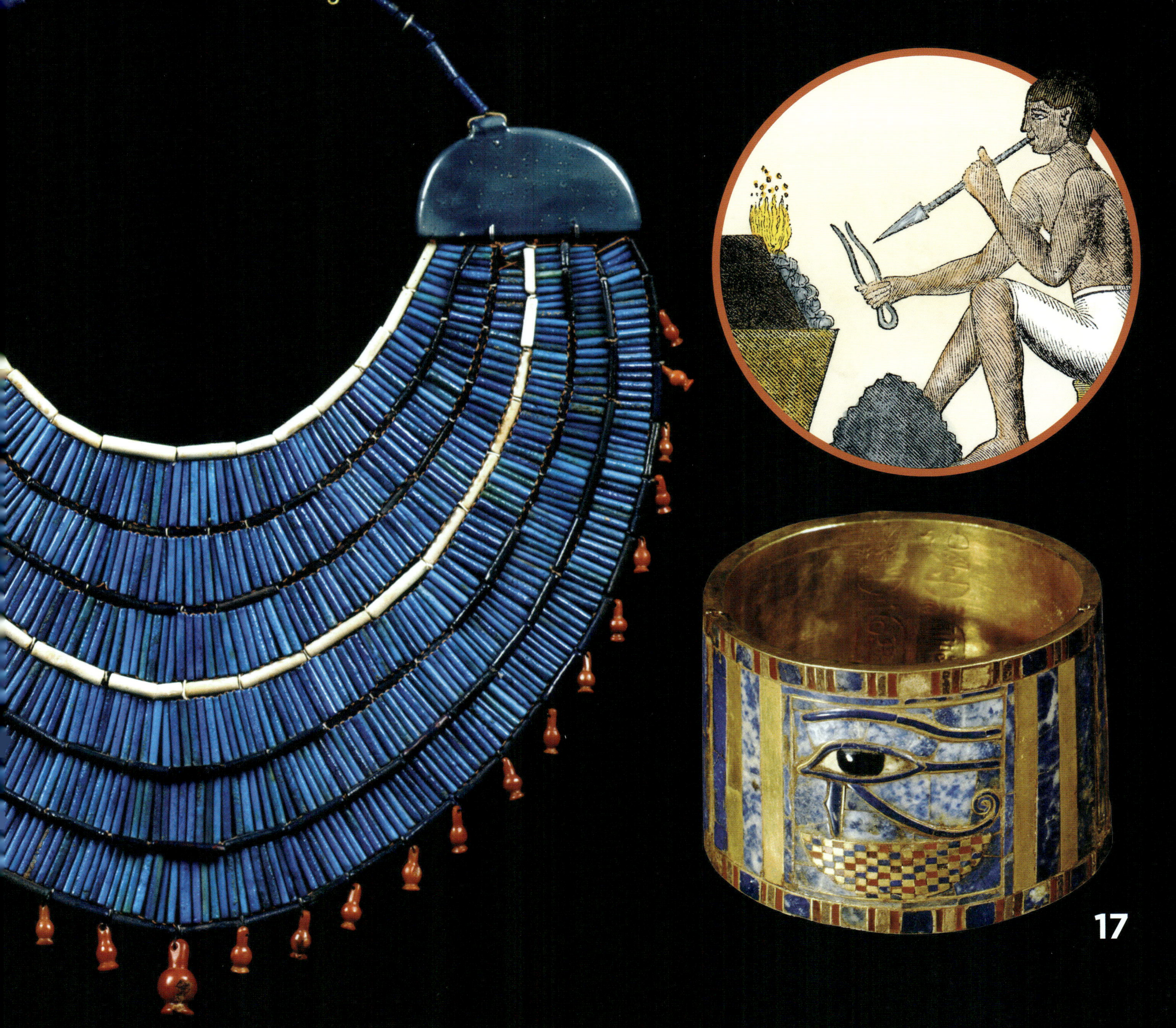

Sculptures

Sculptors carved items of all sizes. **Funerary statues** were smaller and placed in tombs. The Sphinx of Giza was carved from one giant piece of sandstone. It is more than 240 feet (73 m) long!

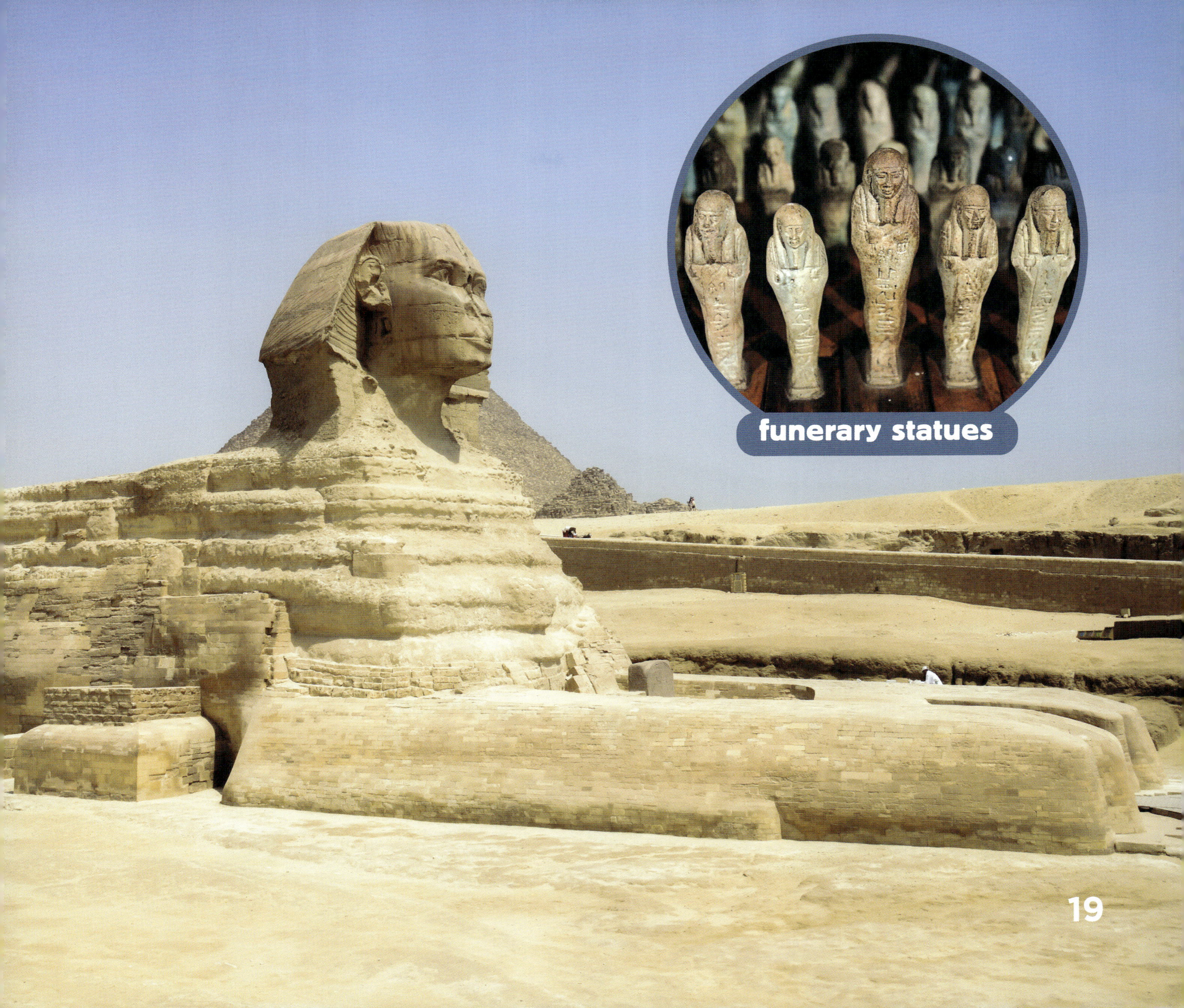

funerary statues

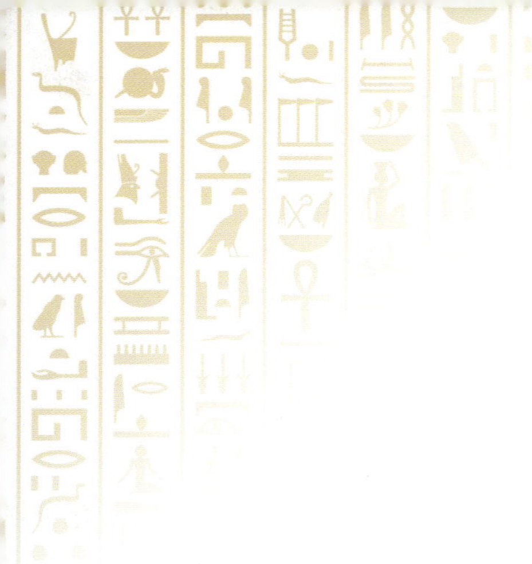

Paintings

Tomb paintings were created by teams of artists. These were **elaborate** scenes from Egyptian life and the world of the gods.

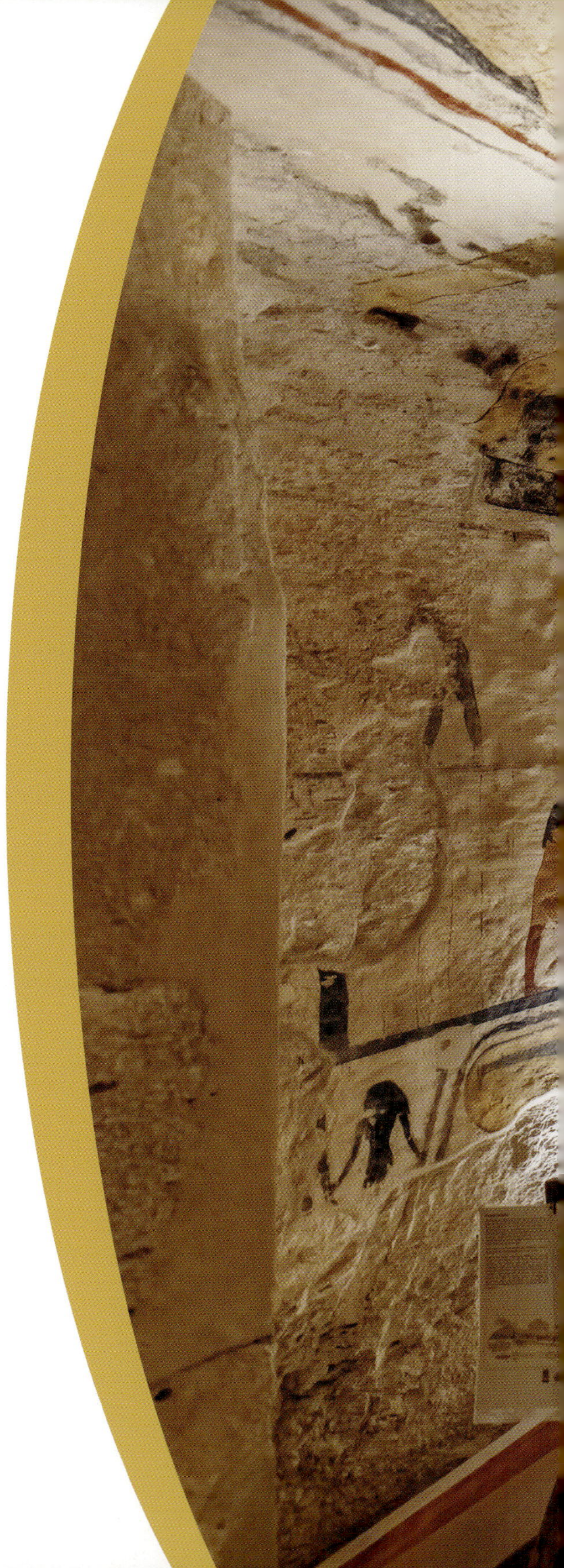

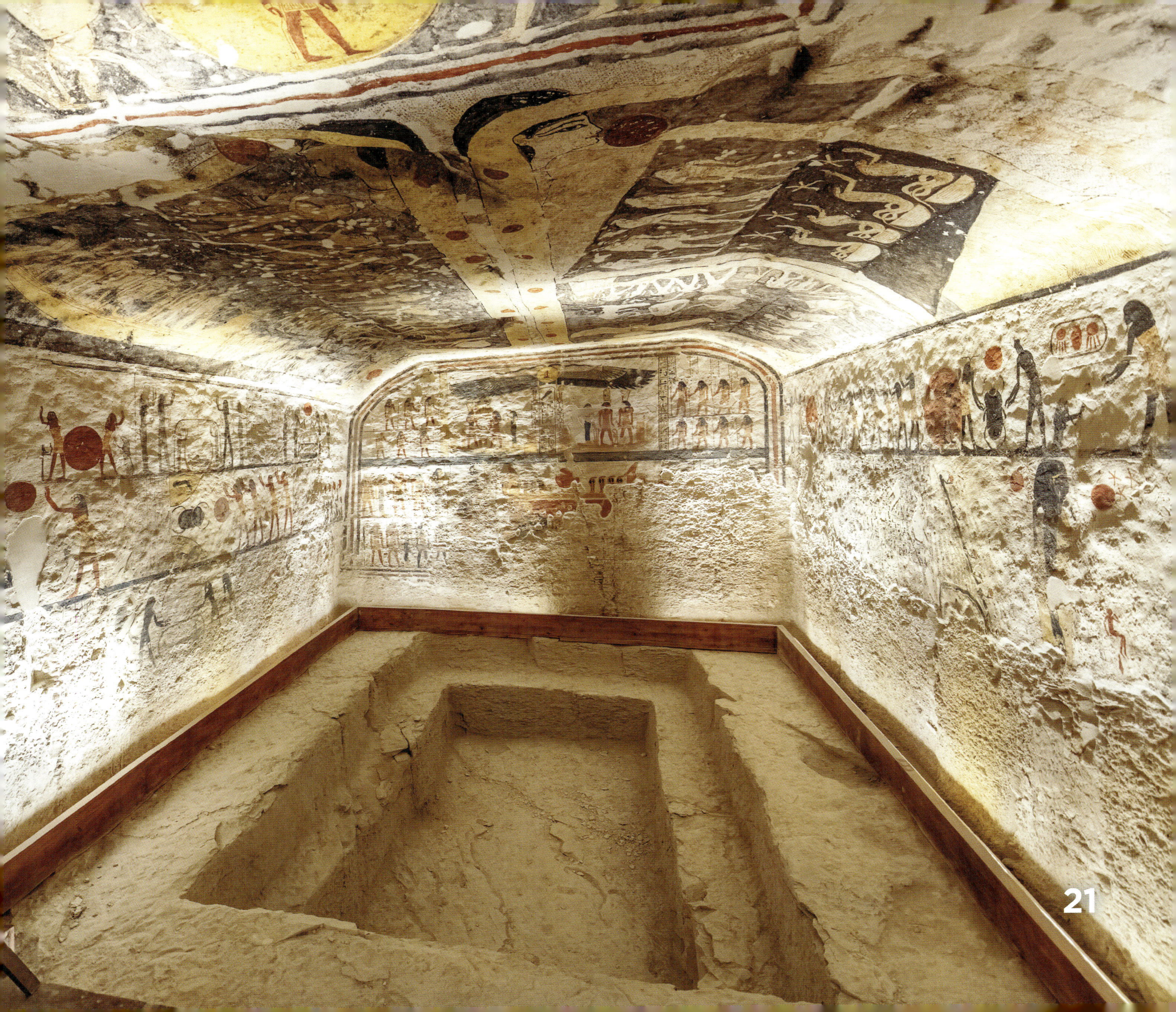

Famous Ancient Egyptian Art

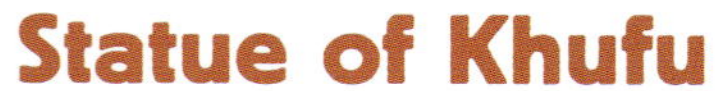

Statue of Khufu

- Discovered in the Temple of Khentyamentiu
- Carved from ivory

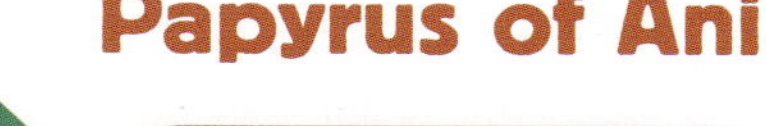

Papyrus of Ani

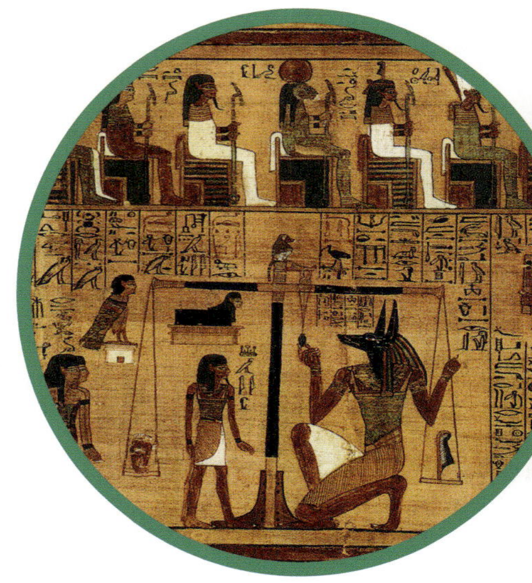

- Discovered in the Tomb of Ani
- One of the most famous examples of the *Book of the Dead*

Bust of Nefertiti

- Discovered at Amarna
- Painted stucco-coated limestone

Vulture collar

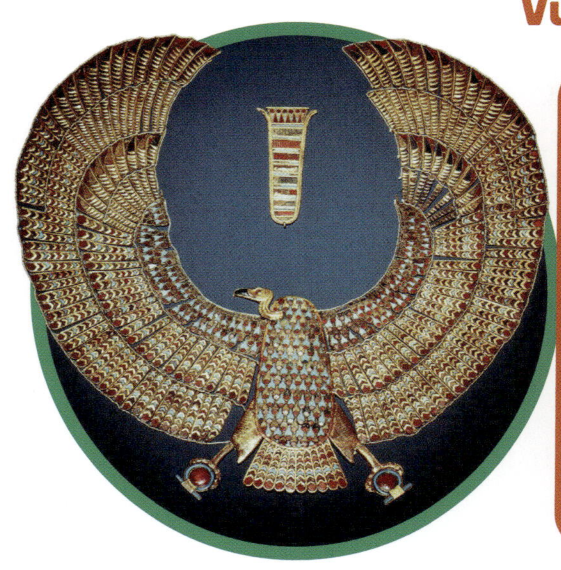

- Discovered around the neck of King Tut's mummy in his tomb
- Composed of gold, colored glass, and **obsidian**

Glossary

artisan – a person skilled in making things, especially by using their hands.

climate – the usual weather conditions in a place.

elaborate – planned or carried out with great care and attention to details.

faience – specifically Egyptian faience, a self-glazing ceramic made mainly of sand or crushed quartz, sodium, and calcium.

funerary statue – a figurine designed to be placed in someone's tomb that could be made from many materials.

glaze – to give a smooth glossy surface to.

obsidian – a dark, shiny volcanic glass, often used in jewelry.

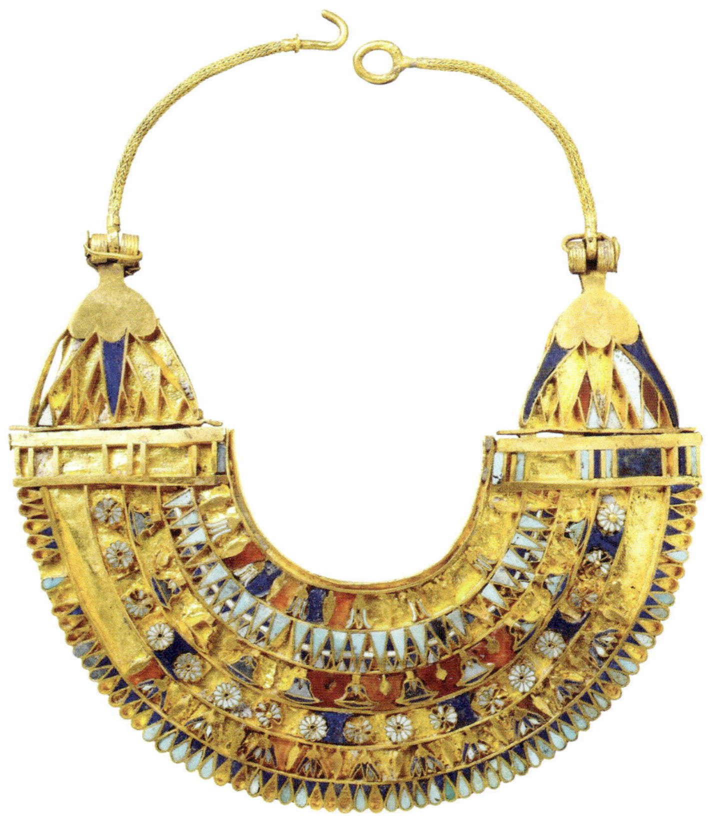

Index